# POLAR BEAR CUBS

## BY DOWNS MATTHEWS
## PHOTOGRAPHS BY DAN GURAVICH

SIMON AND SCHUSTER BOOKS FOR YOUNG READERS
Published by Simon & Schuster Inc., New York

▲▲▲▲▲▲▲▲▲▲▲▲▲▲▲▲▲

SIMON AND SCHUSTER
BOOKS FOR YOUNG READERS
Simon & Schuster Building
Rockefeller Center
1230 Avenue of the Americas
New York, New York 10020

Designed by Malle N. Whitaker.
Manufactured in the United States of America.

10  9  8  7  6  5  4  3  2  1

Library of Congress Cataloging-in-Publication Data
Matthews, Downs.
  Polar bear cubs/Downs Matthews;
  photographs by Dan Guravich.
  Summary: Describes the life of a pair of polar
  bear cubs as they play, explore, and learn to
  hunt with their mother.
  1. Polar bear—Behavior—Juvenile literature.
  2. Polar bear—Development—Juvenile
  literature.   3. Animals—Infancy—Juvenile
  literature.   4. Mammals—Behavior—Juvenile
  literature.   5. Mammals—Development—
  Juvenile literature.   [1. Polar bear.]   I.
  Guravich, Dan, ill.   II. Title.
  QL737.C27M355 1989     599.74′446—dc19
  88-10284

ISBN 0-671-66757-2

icture a place so cold that oceans freeze…a place where tall trees can't grow…a place where the sun never shines in winter nor sets in summer. There is such a place. It is called the Arctic. It is the world of snow and ice at the North Pole. Polar bears live there.

Polar bears are sometimes called ice bears because they are at home on the frozen surface of the Arctic Ocean. Nature has given them the things they need to live and be comfortable in the cold weather. They have warm white coats. The hairs of their fur are hollow to trap heat. They store a thick layer of fat under their skin to keep out the cold.

Polar bears are not herd animals. They stay by themselves. They hunt alone and seldom see each other. But in the spring of each year, male polar bears look for female polar bears to mate with.

The bears mate in April. When a female bear knows she is going to be a mother, she eats many seals and grows fat. In September, she leaves the sea ice and returns to her birthplace. There she searches for a den where her cubs can be born. A den is a cave dug into the frozen earth or a deep snowdrift.

When the female finds a den she likes, she goes inside and settles down. Winter winds blow snow over the entrance to the den. In December, the female gives birth to her cubs.

A female bear usually gives birth to two cubs at a time. When they are born, the cubs are smaller than a human baby. They are only a foot long and weigh a little more than one pound. Fine white hair covers their bodies. Their eyes are closed. Like human babies, they can do nothing for themselves.

But polar bear cubs grow quickly. Their mother feeds them on rich milk. Each day they gain weight. Their fur grows out and becomes thick. In a couple of weeks their eyes open. After two months they learn to walk. They begin to explore their den and learn how it looks and smells.

By March, the male cub weighs thirty pounds. His smaller sister weighs twenty-five pounds. It is time for them to leave the den and learn about the outside world.

Their mother pushes away the snow that covers the entrance to the den. The cubs are bewildered at first. The world is new and strange. They have never seen the sky or felt the wind. The mother lies down and holds her cubs next to her body to keep them warm.

▽ Ptarmigan

△ An Arctic fox in its winter coat.

Each day, the female bear takes her cubs outside. The cubs learn about their world. They see bushy willow trees just three feet tall. White birds called ptarmigan feed like chickens on willow buds. Under the snow, little furry rodents called lemmings live in tunnels they dig. Arctic foxes trot by, hunting the lemmings. White-feathered gyrfalcons and snowy owls fly overhead, looking for ptarmigan to eat. Sometimes herds of caribou pass by. After them come wolves, which feed on caribou.

As the days pass, the polar bear cubs grow stronger and wiser. They learn how to walk in the snow. At first, they slip and slide. They fall and tumble. But their big square paws help them stay on top of the snow's crust. Their claws grow out and help them grip the surface.

When a fox comes close, the mother bear worries. She fears the fox might bite her cubs. She lowers her head and growls. Then she runs at the fox.

The cubs learn by imitating their mother. They growl when their mother growls. When she chases the fox, they follow. When she goes for a walk, her cubs put their feet in her tracks. When she lifts her nose to smell the air, they sniff too. They learn that every animal has its own scent. Soon, the cubs can tell all the animals apart by their smell, even at a distance or in the dark. Their keen noses warn them when danger approaches.

The cubs play in the snow. They stand on their hind legs and wrestle with each other. They run and chase.

Exercise makes them hungry. Their mother scoops a hollow in the snow and sits down. The cubs run to her and nurse. Her milk is so rich that they soon get fat. They no longer feel the cold.

▽ Nursing

Now the days are getting longer. Spring is coming to the Arctic. The female polar bear must catch seals to eat before the sea ice melts and the seals swim away. She hasn't eaten for many months, but she has had to nurse two growing cubs. She is getting thin and hungry. She must have food.

The way to the frozen sea lies over fields of snow. The mother bear leads and her cubs follow, putting their paws in her tracks.

When the cubs grow tired, they complain to their mother with little whines. She stops and lets them nurse. She holds them next to her body while they take a nap. After their nap, they want to play, but their mother won't let them. She snorts, "Chuff! Chuff! Chuff!" It is time to leave, and when their mother walks away, the cubs follow.

As she travels, the cubs' mother sniffs the air. Her keen nose picks up scents of all kinds. She smells foxes, but the cubs are too large now for a fox to hurt them. She smells wolves, and from far away she smells a big male polar bear. That is something to worry about. Adult male bears sometimes kill cubs. She also smells seals, which to her mean food. She walks faster. The cubs trot behind.

When they reach the seashore, the cubs are tired. Their mother takes them behind a low ridge to a spot sheltered from the wind. Little willow trees grow there, close to the ground. The snow lies deep among the willows. She makes a bed for the cubs by digging a hole in the snow. Lying down together, the bears curl up against each other and go to sleep. The wind blows a blanket of snow over them. Underneath, they are snug and comfortable.

When she awakes, the female polar bear raises her
head and sniffs the air. She picks out the scent
of an adult male bear coming toward her. That's bad
news. She wakes her cubs and hurries away. The cubs
must run to keep up.

The mother hopes to avoid the male bear, but he sees
them and follows. Now she knows that she cannot run
away. Encouraging her cubs to stay behind her, she
lowers her head, curls her lip, and shows her teeth. To a
bear, this means anger. The female advances on the male
bear, growling. The male is three times the size of the
female, but he doesn't want a fight. Polar bears are so
big and strong that they could kill each other easily.

The male bear stands still and turns his head away. The female advances with her jaws open and her long teeth showing. She charges at the male bear. He opens his jaws too, but backs away.

As their mother challenges the male bear, the cubs growl and hiss, just as she does.

But the female bear still fears for her cubs. She throws herself at the male and knocks him down. After that, he decides to leave her alone. He jumps to his feet and trots away. The female bear calls to her cubs. They set off again for the frozen sea where they can hunt seals.

At the seashore, the ice is broken and jagged. Chunks
of old ice lie on top of sheets of new ice like building
blocks on a floor. It is uneven and slippery. The female
polar bear moves slowly. She must let her cubs learn to
walk on this new surface or they may fall and hurt
themselves. The bears have hair on the bottoms of their
feet and the pads of their toes have tiny cups in the skin.
These help them walk without slipping.

The female bear raises her head high. She tastes the air. The scent of seals is on it. That means food.

Several kinds of seal make their home in the Arctic Ocean. They swim below the ice and feed on fish and small animals like shrimp. Seals and polar bears are both mammals. They are warm-blooded and breathe air. To breathe, seals sometimes make holes in the ice so they can come to the surface. Where the ice breaks apart, seals crawl out of the water to rest. But they must be careful. To stay fat and healthy, an adult polar bear must catch and eat one seal a week.

▽ Bearded seals sunning themseives by a gap in the sea ice.

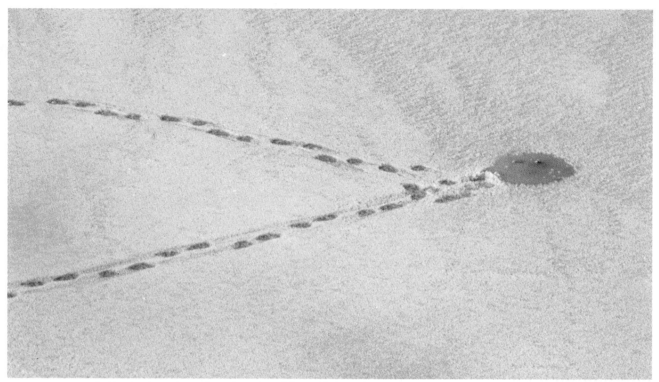

To catch a seal, a bear must be patient and quiet. Seals have good ears and can hear the sound of a bear's foot as it steps on the snow. If a seal hears a bear coming, it will swim away to safety. A bear will sometimes have to wait for many hours by a breathing hole for the seal to return. When the seal comes back, the bear must move quickly to catch it before it can escape.

The female bear leads her cubs to a breathing hole out on the sea ice. She shows them how to move and wait quietly. If they start to play, she spanks them and nips their ears. She must teach them to be patient when they hunt, or they will go hungry.

Eventually, a seal comes to the surface to breathe. The female bear pounces and drags it out onto the ice. She calls to her cubs to come and look at the dead seal and taste its meat.

As the months pass, the cubs continue to grow bigger and stronger. After a year, they know how to catch seals, but they still have much to learn. They are not yet ready to leave their mother. She protects them and teaches them how to stay alive and healthy in their harsh world.

The cubs sleep and play and explore new things. At the same time, they practice the skills they will need when they grow up and have to look after themselves.

By the time they are two years old, polar bear cubs can live alone in the Arctic. Their mother has taught them how to walk over snow and ice and swim in the cold water. They know how to make a bed in the snow and keep warm during the winter storms, and they have learned the ways of seals and how to hunt for them. They know how to wash after eating and keep themselves clean. It is time for them to leave their mother and go their separate ways.

When he is eight years old, the male cub will mate with an adult female and become a father. When she is six, the female cub will be old enough to find a mate and have cubs of her own. She will teach them how to live in the wintry Arctic world, just as her mother taught her.